NATIONAL GEOGRAPHIC

Ladders

AFRICAN SAVANNA

2 Elephant Orphanage *Science Article*
by Suzanne Sherman

10 Living on the African Savanna *Science Article*
by Suzanne Sherman

18 Animal Architects *Science Article*
by Suzanne Sherman

22 Saving Big Cats *Nonfiction Narrative*
by Suzanne Sherman

32 Discuss

D1286662

Elephant Orphanage

by Suzanne Sherman

Four-year-old Kilaguni rushes toward Kibo, a three-year-old. They playfully wrap their trunks together and bump heads before breaking for a midday feeding.

Kibo and Kilaguni came to the David Sheldrick Wildlife Trust's elephant nursery in Kenya when they were infants. Two-week-old Kibo was found trapped in a well. Six-month-old Kilaguni had injuries to his tail and ears. Their mothers could not be found. Injured and orphaned African elephants can heal and grow into healthy adults in the Wildlife Trust's Orphans' Project.

The nursery provides the elephants with food and shelter. It also provides relationships, which are key to their survival. Elephants are highly social animals that can't survive without a family. In the wild, young elephants are raised by the females of their families. Within these groups, they form strong bonds that last their whole lives, up to 70 years. They even show signs of grief when a member of their family dies.

Each elephant in the orphanage has its own personality. Some elephants are stressed from losing their family, which may cause them to act out. But most of the elephants will make a full recovery.

Social bonds are key to an elephant's well-being.

Where Are the Adults?

More than a million elephants once roamed the continent of Africa. Now there are only about 500,000 elephants. People have taken much of the elephants' land for farming. People also **poach,** or illegally kill, elephants for meat or their ivory tusks. Many people want objects made from ivory, such as this carving, which has led to more elephant poaching.

ELEPHANT POPULATION DECLINE

Less than half a century ago, there were an estimated 1.3 million African elephants. Habitat loss and poaching has brought the number down to around 500,000.

1979

Elephant tusks are taken from poachers and burned. That shows the government's resolve to end poaching.

In 1989, a ban was placed on ivory trade to prevent poaching. The ban seemed to be working. Some wild elephant herds began to come back. But ivory from elephants that died of natural causes could still be sold. In China, Thailand, and the Philippines, ivory is carved into religious statues and charms. The value of these objects has made the price of ivory soar. Now, greedy dealers buy and sell any ivory they can get. They don't seem to care if elephants were poached for it. People break the law against poaching, and many get away with it.

Elephant tusks are enlarged incisor teeth. Males and females use tusks mostly for defense. The tusks continue to grow throughout the elephant's life. An adult elephant can have tusks up to six feet long. So poachers hunt adult elephants. This leaves many young elephants alone in the wild. This is the case for many of the orphans of the Wildlife Trust.

  2012

One white elephant represents 100,000 elephants in the wild.

Growing Up

In the Orphans' Project, raising elephants is a three-part process. First, elephants go to the nursery. Then, they go to a rehabilitation center. Finally, they begin the transition back into the wild. Baby elephants depend on their mothers' milk for the first two years of their lives. In the nursery, human keepers feed the baby elephants a milk formula.

The project's founder, Daphne Sheldrick, and her husband developed the formula themselves. It took them decades to get the ingredients just right.

Other elephants and human keepers become an orphan's new family. Older female elephants look after the younger ones. Keepers stay with the babies

Caring nursery keepers act as stand-ins for the baby elephants' family members.

24 hours a day. They feed the elephants, keep them warm with blankets, and give them time for social play. At night, keepers sleep next to them.

When the orphans no longer depend only on milk, they are moved to a rehabilitation center in Tsavo East National Park. At this stage, the keepers start taking them out to the bush where they learn to nibble on natural vegetation. But vegetation is not the only thing the orphans discover in the wild. There they will meet wild elephants for the first time.

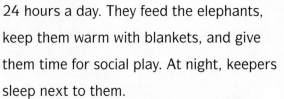

Daphne Sheldrick

Back Into the Wild

The final step of the Orphans' Project is introducing the elephants back into the wild. This happens only when an orphan chooses a wild family to join. The elephants are torn between joining the wild group and leaving their orphanage family.

They may leave and come back many times before they are fully wild again. Eight to ten years can pass before they leave for good.

The Orphan's Project has been very successful. Most of the orphans that survive recover and live as healthy adults.

Orphan and wild elephants mingle over a fence.

So far, more than a hundred elephants have been returned to the wild. Elephants are known for their great memories. They never forget their keepers. One female came back many years after living in the wild to show the keepers her new baby!

At the time of this writing, Kibo and Kilaguni are doing well in the rehabilitation center. When they are ready, Kibo and Kilaguni will once again roam the African **savanna.**

Check In Why aren't young elephants released into the wild as soon as their wounds are healed?

Living on the AFR

by Suzanne Sherman

Over a million wildebeests migrate north from Tanzania to Kenya and back each year.

In the heat of the **savanna,** the streams have been drying for weeks. The grasses have been turning brown. A booming sound fills the air. It is the pounding of millions of wildebeests' hooves. The animals are making their way across the African savanna. These horned mammals travel a thousand miles each year. They are in search of fresh water to drink and green grass to graze on.

The African savanna **ecosystem** has wet and dry seasons. An ecosystem is made up of all the organisms in an area as well as conditions such as temperature and rainfall. Plants and animals on the African savanna have adapted to extreme heat and drought.

ICAN SAVANNA

Savanna covers almost half the surface of Africa.

Some animals go underground to escape the heat. Others, such as wildebeests, migrate in the dry season.

Tall grasses die back during the dry season. Their tiny buds stay alive near the surface of the soil. Acacia trees' deep roots help them reach water, and their small, waxy leaves help store the water.

The living things of the African savanna are connected. For example, as the wildebeests cross the land, they cut the grasses. They fertilize the soil with their droppings.

They also provide food for the crocodiles, lions, and cheetahs. Connections such as these allow many species to survive here.

MEET the WILDLIFE

The African savanna ecosystem is home to some of the most amazing plants and animals on the planet.

cheetah

zebra

baobab

secretary bird

white rhinoceros

black mamba

termite mound

acacia

giraffe

red grass

BAOBAB The baobab tree stores water for the dry season in its trunk. Its small leaves limit water loss. Its thick bark protects it from fire.

RED GRASS Red grass is food for grazers on the savanna. The long bristles of its flower twirl when wet. Its seeds flutter to the ground.

SECRETARY BIRD The tall feathers on the head of a secretary bird look like the pens that secretaries used to use. These birds pant to keep cool in the heat.

WHITE RHINOCEROS White rhinos are really tan or gray. They keep cool by bathing in mud. Mud is a natural sunblock and bug repellent.

BLACK MAMBA Black mambas are among the world's fastest snakes. They are also among the deadliest. Their deadly venom can kill any animal.

TERMITE MOUND Huge termite mounds took centuries to build from mud and termite saliva. Termite mounds are good for the soil and animals use them, too. Lions and cheetahs use them as lookout points. Small animals on the savanna use them for shade.

CHEETAH A cheetah's spotted coat helps it blend into the dry grasses. It can reach 96 km/h (60 mph) in three seconds!

ACACIA Acacia trees provide shade on the savanna. Pairs of long, sharp thorns keep most animals from eating its leaves.

GIRAFFE Giraffes have tough, purple tongues! They munch leaves on the acacia trees without getting a scratch. Giraffes give the trees an umbrella shape as they eat the lowest leaves.

ZEBRA The pattern of stripes on a zebra can confuse its predators. Each zebra has a unique pattern of stripes, like a fingerprint.

FOOD for ALL

The story of life in the African savanna ecosystem begins with the sun. Once its energy reaches Earth, it fuels one living thing after another in a series of relationships called a **food chain.**

Sunlight energy hits the leaf of an acacia tree. The tree is a **producer,** so it uses the energy to make its own food. Some of the energy is stored. But then an elephant comes along. An elephant is a **consumer** that cannot make its own food. It eats the leaves and uses the tree's stored energy for its own survival.

The African savanna has the most types of herbivores, or plant-eating consumers, in the world. Grazers eat low plants and

GRASS
producer

HYENA
consumer

grasses. Browsers eat from trees and shrubs. Elephants, wildebeests, zebras, rhinos, giraffes, and warthogs are all herbivores of the savanna.

Lions, leopards, cheetahs, and wild dogs are all carnivores of the savanna. These consumers get all their energy by eating other animals.

Scavengers get their energy from eating dead animals. Hyenas, vultures, and jackals are scavengers. Decomposers use the remaining energy. Bacteria and fungi are decomposers. They break down any leftovers and release nutrients into the soil.

This chain is just one possible path energy can take through the savanna ecosystem. All the different food chains make up a **food web.**

TREES and SHRUBS
producers

VULTURE
consumer

ELEPHANT
consumer

LION
consumer

TEAM WORK

Think of all the savanna relationships you have read about so far. These relationships are an important part of the savanna ecosystem. Some species of the African savanna have formed unusual partnerships.

warthog + mongoose

The warthog lies down and a group of banded mongooses come running. They climb over the warthog's skin. They eat insects that the warthog would not be able to clear away by itself.

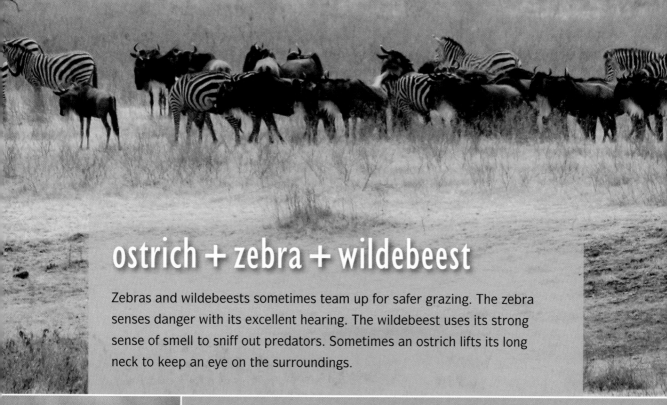

ostrich + zebra + wildebeest

Zebras and wildebeests sometimes team up for safer grazing. The zebra senses danger with its excellent hearing. The wildebeest uses its strong sense of smell to sniff out predators. Sometimes an ostrich lifts its long neck to keep an eye on the surroundings.

giraffe + oxpecker

A giraffe and red-billed oxpeckers form a team. The oxpeckers get a meal of ticks and insects and the giraffe gets cleaned of pests. When the giraffe is asleep, and a predator is near, the oxpeckers chirp and flap their wings to wake the giraffe.

Check In | Explain three different strategies that wildlife use to survive on the savanna.

LOOK AROUND

the room you're in. The walls, floor, and furniture were all created by people. We change our **ecosystem** when we build structures. Other living things change their environments, too. Male weaver birds build detailed nests, hoping to attract females.

WOVEN HOMES

The village weaver is a noisy and colorful bird. It builds its nests on trees near rivers in the African **savanna** and other places. The nests are woven out of leaves, grasses, and reeds. Sometimes more than a hundred nests hang from one tree. When the male finishes building the nest, he hangs upside down, flutters his wings, and chatters loudly. He is showing off his work to females.

A male village weaver shows off his creation.

Animal A

by Suzanne Sherman

A social weaver nest may have up to 100 entrances. They are located at the bottom of the nest.

The social weaver builds a giant nest in an acacia tree. As many as 400 birds may live in one nest. The nest is like an apartment building. Each family has its own entrance that leads to its own sleeping area. A thick roof holds in heat at night and keeps the nest cool during the day. Sometimes an African pygmy falcon will move into one of the rooms of a social weaver nest. The falcon feeds on reptiles that prey on the birds. In return, it gets a "free" place to stay.

rchitects

SWEET DIGS

The naked mole rat lives its whole life in tunnels under the ground in Eastern Africa. These odd rodents have no ears and almost no eyes. They have fine hairs that act like whiskers to help them feel their surroundings. Using these hairs to "see," they run backward through their tunnels as well as forward.

Naked mole rats use their long front teeth to dig large burrows. Hundreds of family members live in them. Tunnels connect a variety of rooms. In a nursery, the queen tends to the pups. In a kitchen, food is stored and eaten. There is even a bathroom! The above-ground temperature varies, but the temperature inside the burrow stays at 30°C (86°F).

The naturalist who first discovered the naked mole rat thought it was diseased because of its lack of fur.

THE NAKED TRUTH

Naked mole rats are not moles or rats. They are related to porcupines, chinchillas, and guinea pigs.

Naked mole rats live in large colonies with a queen, soldiers, and workers.

When digging, several naked mole rats will line up in a row. They sweep the dirt back like on an assembly line.

Naked mole rats do not have sweat glands to help them cool off or fat to keep them warm.

Naked mole rats don't get cancer. Scientists want to learn why.

The skin of a naked mole rat doesn't sense pain.

Naked mole rats live up to 28 years.

Check In   How do the homes of the weaver bird and naked mole rat help them survive in the African savanna climate?

SAVING BIG CATS

by Suzanne Sherman

BEVERLY AND DERECK JOUBERT are award-winning wildlife photographers, filmmakers, and conservationists. They are also National Geographic Explorers. They have observed and documented African wildlife for nearly 30 years. They have produced nature films and books. Beverly Joubert took most of the photos on the following pages.

The Jouberts document big cats and other African animals. Their goal is to show these animals in their natural environment. They want to help others understand and value them.

The Jouberts take care not to disturb the animals they are documenting. Sometimes they must be patient and wait. Other times they must be brave.

They have had to swim through crocodile-infested water, face an angry elephant, and watch out for all kinds of pests.

The Jouberts believe the challenges of their work help them show what animal life is truly like in Africa. In 2003, the Jouberts met an eight-day-old leopard. They followed her as she grew, learned to hunt, and parted with her mother. They named her Legadema, or "light from the sky." Legadema taught them that conservation is about individual animals with lives and personalities.

A mother leopard grooms her cub.

Launching an Initiative

Beverly and Dereck understand lions as well as anyone could. And they know the future of the lion is in great danger.

The lion population has dropped from 450,000 to around 20,000 in the last 50 years. At this rate, lions will be gone from the wild forever. People are destroying the lions' habitat. **Poachers** are a threat as well. Cattle herders also kill lions to defend their livestock.

People have caused the lions' downfall. So the Jouberts believe that people can bring lions back.

The Jouberts' mission is to conserve large cats and other African wildlife. They work with Great Plains Conservation. This company buys large areas of land in Africa to preserve the big cats' habitat.

National Geographic and the Jouberts have started the Big Cats Initiative. The goal is to save the big cats in Africa and elsewhere. The Big Cats Initiative raises awareness and funding to support conservation.

The Jouberts' vehicle is also their studio, office, kitchen, and sleeping quarters.

Why Big Cats Matter

As top predators, lions are a **keystone species.** Like a center stone that supports an arch, a keystone species supports the rest of the **ecosystem.** Big cats keep populations of grazers from getting too big and keep them migrating. If grazers overpopulate the land and stop migrating, the plants and soil would be affected. All the other animals that depend on the plants and soil would be affected, too.

Top predators are necessary to the health of an ecosystem. How do we know? Just look at Yellowstone National Park in the United States. Gray wolves are a keystone species of this ecosystem. They were killed off in the 1800s. Without wolves to hunt them, elk stood out in the open and grazed on trees. The trees near stream edges disappeared. As

a result, other animals lost their habitat. The removal of the gray wolf affected the entire ecosystem. This top predator has since been reintroduced to the Yellowstone ecosystem. The natural ecosystem has also made a comeback. Big cats are likely to be just as important to the African **savanna** ecosystem.

Local communities need top predators, too. Tourists from around the world come to see lions and cheetahs. This industry brings in $80 billion a year. A large part of that goes to African communities. Without big cats drawing in the tourists, the money would be lost.

Traditional fences leave Maasai livestock open to attack. In another Big Cat Initiative program, Maasai are provided with improved fencing to keep predators out.

Finding Peace

One Big Cat Initiative program is working to improve the relationship between the Maasai people of Kenya and lions. The Maasai have lived in East Africa for hundreds of years. Cattle are central to Maasai life. The people protect, feed, and care for the cattle.

The cattle provide milk, blood, and hides for them to use. The cattle are traded with other groups for goods. Maasai people view cattle as a sacred gift.

Maasai houses are temporary and built of sticks and cattle dung. The people often travel to find the best pasture for their livestock. They often move near Kenya's parks and reserves. Lions and other predators live here.

A Maasai herder uses a radio receiver to track the activity of lions.

Maasai build pens for their livestock. These pens give the animals little protection. Many cattle and goats fall prey to lions. In turn, the Maasai kill the lions. There are less than 200 lions left in the Maasai region.

The Maasai depend on their cattle to survive. So the Big Cat Initiative gives money to herders who have lost livestock to lions.

The program also pays the Maasai to protect the lions. Many lions wear radio collars around their necks. The Maasai keep track of the lions' activity. They use cell phones to tell other herders where to guide their livestock. They also alert authorities when they spot hunters. Far fewer lions have been killed in the area since the program began.

Making a Movie

While watching big cats, Beverly and Dereck Joubert have seen complex relationships. They've seen death, but they have also seen animals survive against all odds.

When we appreciate the life of another creature, we reflect on our ability to overcome life's struggles, our relationships, and our thoughts on life and death.

In 2011, the Jouberts launched a movie called *The Last Lions: An Incredible True Story of Survival*. They hope to raise awareness, support, and funding for Big Cat Initiative projects, as a result of this movie.

"We know that our souls, the very essence of what makes us human, would shrivel if they disappeared."
— Dereck Joubert

The movie is a tale of a determined lioness. They named her Ma di Tau, or "Mother of Lions." Ma di Tau bravely faces challenges as she struggles to keep herself and her cubs alive.

The movie's purpose is to honestly show what may truly be the last of the wild lions. *The Last Lions* is the Jouberts' call to action.

The Jouberts feel that losing Africa's big cats would mean more than losing an animal and its ecosystem. It would mean losing an animal that has been a symbol of bravery and strength for thousands of years.

A FILM BY CELEBRATED WILDLIFE FILMMAKERS **DERECK & BEVERLY JOUBERT**

THE MOST POWERFUL
FORCE IN NATURE IS A
MOTHER'S LOVE

THE
**LAST
LIONS**

AN INCREDIBLE **TRUE** STORY OF SURVIVAL

AS TOLD BY ACADEMY AWARD® WINNER **JEREMY IRONS**
ONLY IN THEATERS STARTING **FEBRUARY 2011**

Check In   How do you think the Jouberts' film can make a difference to the big cats?

Discuss

1. What connections can you make among the four pieces in this book?

2. Think about and describe two ways people affect African elephants.

3. What effects might wildebeests have on the savanna ecosystem if all the big cats were killed off?

4. What are the main producers of the African savanna? Why are they called producers?

5. Describe some ways social weaver birds interact with living and nonliving things in their environment.

6. What else do you want to learn about the African savanna? How could you learn more?